A Very SCREAMING GOAT HALLOWEEN

A Very SCREAMING GOAT HALLOWEEN

WRITTEN BY
Jessie Oleson Moore

ILLUSTRATED BY
Lee Hodges

RP MINIS
PHILADELPHIA

RP Minis®
Hachette Book Group
1290 Avenue of the Americas, New York, NY 10104
www.runningpress.com
@Running_Press

First Edition: July 2025

Published by RP Minis, an imprint of Hachette Book Group, Inc. The RP Minis name and logo is a registered trademark of Hachette Book Group, Inc.

Contact specialmarkets@hbgusa.com regarding special discounts for bulk purchases.

Design by Tanvi Baghele

ISBN: 978-0-7624-8974-9

Made in Dongguan, China (HKD) 06/26 #02

Get Ready for the G.H.O.A.T.

(GOATIEST HALLOWEEN OF ALL TIME)

Screaming goats are back, and they're brimming with spooky Halloween spirit! This mini kit is your gateway to the G.H.O.A.T. (Goatiest Halloween of All Time), featuring a mini goat that's equal parts trick *and* treat. Sure, it's as cute as a candy corn kernel, dressed up like a little witch and sitting pretty atop a pumpkin base. But it also screams like the devil over bone-tingling tunes! (Go ahead, press the button. We'll wait.)

But the greatest and goat-iest of all Halloweens doesn't

stop there. In this book, you'll discover the origin stories of iconic Halloween goats, instructions on how to dress a mini goat for Halloween (not as simple as you might think), and ideas for throwing a goat-themed Halloween party that's bound to be a scream. Let's get goating—er, going.

Meet the HALLOWEEN Goats

Here they are—all your favorite Halloween characters reimagined as goats!

WITCH GOAT

Look up in the air! Is it a bird? A plane? No, it's a screaming goat witch! Legend has it that one day, a goat was wearing its favorite pointy hat and taking a casual walk with its black cat bestie in an enchanted wood. When the goat came across a broom on the path, it started gnawing on the handle, as goats are wont to do. Little did it know this was an enchanted broom, and it immediately took off skyward with the goat still clamped on! The cat tried to rescue the goat but ended up being taken along for the ride, too. If you look up in the sky on Halloween eve, you might just see a witchy goat and its cat trying to shake free of their enchanted broom.

ZOMBIE GOAT

Baaah-rains! Once upon a time, there was a goat who became a zombie (we won't trouble you with the gruesome details). The newly zombified goat screamed in horror when it learned that "traditional" zombies seek to prolong their afterlife by consuming actual brains (yuck). Rather than lowering itself to such gauche behavior, the zombie goat chose to enhance its *own* brain—by devouring books. While you don't have to worry about a zombie goat eating your brains, its appetite for books is insatiable. So if you see one coming, hide those precious pages!

FRANKEN-GOAT

A long time ago, in a toy factory, a mischievous assembler gave an adorable goat toy the ability to scream instead of the typical squeak mechanism. This gave all the other workers (and goat toys) quite a scare! The screaming goat was immediately dubbed Franken-goat and was ostracized by the other squeaky goat toys. Poor misunderstood Franken-goat went into hiding to avoid being shipped off to the land of misfit toys and is rarely seen today. If you do happen upon the elusive Franken-goat, don't worry for your safety. Despite the unholy sound it emits, it's actually quite friendly.

GHOST GOAT

Baaah—er, boo! As traditional goat lore goes, ghost goats appear in the afterlife when they have unfinished business in the earthly life, whether it's a partially finished meal or not using up all their prepaid goat yoga sessions. Ghost goats are pretty darned cute—until they open their mouths and let out their signature bloodcurdling scream. Related: You'll definitely know if a ghost goat is haunting your house.

PUMPKIN GOAT

As legend has it, there was once a goat that was so fond of pumpkin spice lattes that it refused all other nourishment. After several seasons of a solely-PSL diet, the goat began to turn orange and round. Before long, it had turned into an unusual goat-pumpkin hybrid, proving the adage that you are what you eat (or in this case, drink). Despite its unorthodox appearance, the pumpkin goat is mostly sugar and spice—although the screaming is a little less nice.

SKELE-GOAT

One day a goat was swinging so high on a swing that it flippec over the swing set. That's about when its insides flipped to the outside, revealinc its skeleton to the world. (For those old enough to remember, Skele-goat's story does indeed echo the cartoon "Inside-Out Boy" from the 1980s. Not familiar? Go ahead, look it up.) Like Franken-goat, the skeleton goat is friendly and somewhat shy, though you wouldn't know it from its frequent screaming.

GUSSY UP YOUR GOATS:

HOW TO DRESS A GOAT FOR HALLOWEEN

Dressing up a mini goat in an adorable Halloween costume is an inimitable life experience. If and when the opportunity avails itself, you need to be prepared. Here's how to do it:

Adopt the Right Mindset

You'll never get that goat into a Halloween costume with the wrong attitude. Believing you can do it is the first step toward manifestation. Repeat this mantra: *I ain't afraid of no goats!*

Wear Headphones

Goats can scream, remember? Protect your precious ears!

BAHHHHHH!

Choose the Perfect Costume

Traditional Halloween costumes are always a great choice. For example, you can use a roll of toilet paper to create a quick mummy goat costume or a sheet with cutouts for a simple ghost getup. Of course, you could *also* consider Billy the Kid, Vincent van Goat, or the Karate Kid. You get the idea.

Ready, Set, Goat!

Even with all the excellent tips listed here, there's probably going to be some "negotiation" as you wrangle your goat into a costume. Be prepared to wrestle and possibly to be screamed at or kicked.

Remember: You'll be rewarded with an alarmingly adorable mini goat in a Halloween costume. Be sure to take videos and/or pics: They might just propel you to viral social media glory.

How to Throw a GOAT-THEMED Halloween Party

Make sure your party is the G.H.O.A.T. by following these tips:

Get the Goat Theme Going Early

Let would-be partygoers know in advance that the theme of the Halloween party is Screaming Goats, and they are expected to wear costumes. While goat-inspired costumes are encouraged, they are not required.

Goaty Greetings

It's always kind to greet guests as they arrive. But instead of saying something boring like "Welcome" or "Trick or Treat," press the button on your mini goat to scream a welcome to each and every guest. Let's goat this party started!

Candy, Candy, Candy! (And Other Food, Too)

Did you know that goats have four stomachs? Help your friends feed their inner goat with all the festive Halloween favorites, like fun-size candy bars, candy corn, and candy pumpkins. You can also serve kitschy concoctions like pigs in a blanket dressed like mummies or deviled eggs decorated like googly eyes.

You've Goata Decorate

The right décor is what separates a ho-hum goat-themed party from an unfor*goat*able Halloween soirée. In addition to Halloween decorations, consider setting the mood with a few tastefully placed hay bales and several hundred screaming Halloween goat figurines.

Get On Down with Your Baaad Self

Keep the vibe high with a playlist jammed with upbeat Halloween hits. It's up to you if you want to encourage guests to dance like goats.

Party Activities

No goats, no glory! Channel some fun and friendly competition with these screaming goat-approved activities:

- Have a Halloween costume contest (winner gets a screaming Halloween goat!)
- Bob for apples
- Pin the tail on the goat

- Goat piñata
- Tell spooky stories (bonus points if they involve goats)
- Replace one word in famous movie or song titles with "goat" and let the hilarity ensue

Goaty Gifts and Party Favors

Don't let your guests leave empty handed—give them a little keepsake to remember their first (possibly only) ever goat-themed Halloween party. You might not be able to give every guest an actual mini goat, but mini bags of candy tied with a festive ribbon are the next best thing.